How to Answer a Fool

How to Answer a Fool

Answering Foolish People Wisely- A Guaranteed Stress Reliever

Marquinn and Marlon Carson

authorHOUSE®

AuthorHouse™
1663 Liberty Drive
Bloomington, IN 47403
www.authorhouse.com
Phone: 1-800-839-8640

First published by AuthorHouse   4/26/2011

ISBN: 978-1-4567-6842-3 (sc)
ISBN: 978-1-4567-6844-7 (hc)
ISBN: 978-1-4567-6843-0 (e)

Printed in the United States of America

Any people depicted in stock imagery provided by Thinkstock are models, and such images are being used for illustrative purposes only. Certain stock imagery © Thinkstock.

This book is printed on acid-free paper.

This book is dedicated to our Lord and Savior Jesus Christ for giving us the wisdom and the understanding to write this book.

Also to our wonderful mother and father, who both went home to be with the Lord in the year 2009.

Special thanks to our wives and families for all their love and support.

Also to our pastor, Bishop MacArthur Jackson, for giving us the opportunity to teach and preach and grow as ministers of the gospel.

Contents

Answer not a fool according to his folly,
lest thou also be like unto him.
–Proverbs 26:4

Answer a fool according to his folly, lest he
be wise in his own conceit.
–Proverbs 26: 5

Introduction

God in his infinite wisdom thought it so important that we understand how to deal with foolish people, and how not to become foolish ourselves, that he gave us over eighty scriptures to help us with this process. The reality is that in just about every aspect of our lives we will encounter foolish people. It is a wise thing to try to avoid them. As Proverbs 14:7 tells us, "Go from the presence of a foolish man, when thou perceivest not in him the lips of knowledge." In some situations this will not be possible, however, simply because that foolish person from whom you want to distance yourself could be a family member, a friend, or a coworker. This book will show you forty-six God-inspired communication principles that will teach you how to answer a fool effectively, because knowing how to answer a fool effectively and wisely will be a guaranteed stress reliever. In Proverbs 15:23 we learn, "A man hath joy by the answer of his mouth," which simply means that knowing how to answer foolish people wisely can become an art that is easy for you, rather than a struggle. Then you will be free to focus all your attention and energy on fulfilling your God-given purpose without being deceived, manipulated, and distracted by foolish people.

Proverbs 10:23 It is as sport to a fool to do mischief: but a man of understanding hath wisdom.

Chapter One

Justifying Your Motives

The ability to justify your motives is something that you need. It is a principle that everyone must understand. In this chapter you will learn how to make yourself clear and how not to leave yourself open or in a position to be misunderstood, because a fool will misunderstand what you have to say on purpose. A fool wants to take what you have to say and substitute his or her own reason for why you said what you said, but we must not let anyone do this. We must be wise enough to recognize the deception in the conversation and quickly let the other person know that we know. By doing so, you will stop the person in his or her tracks because such manipulation only works on those who are not wise enough to see it.

Now let me explain to you what it means to justify your motives. In essence it means protecting the intention behind what you are saying or what you have said and not letting anyone misjudge your motives, thereby causing you to be misunderstood. This is how a fool will try to deceive you. The first thing he or she will do is to listen to what you have to say. Let's say you were talking to a small crowd, and you made the statement that you don't like sports or politics without justifying your motives. The first thing a foolish person is going to assume or think is that what you are really saying is that there is something wrong or bad with sports and politics, which will cause you to be misjudged and misunderstood, simply because you didn't know how to protect your motives from a fool even having the chance to misjudge your motives. To say it another way: don't leave yourself open around a fool. The statement that was made was a preference statement, not a good-or-bad statement; it is a statement of what you like or don't like, but as the speaker, you have to convey that to the people who are listening to you or run the risk of being misjudged.

There is always a foolish person waiting for you to give him or her the opportunity to misjudge you, so you have to decide whether you're going to be misjudged, not them. Make the same statements, but with completeness. Finish by justifying your motives, and don't leave yourself open; shut the door behind every preference statement you make. **Here is the correct way to make your statement: "I don't like sports or politics, but that's not to say that there is something wrong with sports or politics, it's only to say that I don't like sports or politics.**

That's how you justify your motives; you simply leave no room for a foolish person to misjudge your motives. So now you know how not to let your preference statements be turned into good-or-bad statements by a foolish person who is up to no good.

Proverbs 12:15 The way of a fool is right in his own eyes: but he that hearkeneth unto counsel is wise.

Chapter Two

When Foolish People Express Their Desires for the Wrong Reason

This chapter is another piece of the puzzle in knowing how and when to stop a foolish person if he or she expresses desires for the wrong reason. Now, you may be wondering how people express their desires for the wrong reason and why would they want to. If they did, how would you know? By knowing the ways of a fool and having spiritual discernment, you will always know, and you will not feel good about what is being said because the No. 1 reason that a fool will tell you how he or she feels is to try to escape responsibility. But why do they need you to escape their responsibility? It's simple. Foolish, lazy people want to feel good about escaping their personal responsibility, so they look for cosigners to go along with them to make them feel good about making poor choices. Let me explain to you how a foolish person will try to make you his or her cosigner. The first thing such people will do is express how they feel about their responsibility. They might say, "I don't feel like going to work today; I wish I could just stay in bed" or "I don't want to go to school to get my education" or "I wish I could just stay at home and watch the game instead of going to church." Now these statements are basically okay because they express the way a person may feel sometimes, but with the wrong intentions behind them they can turn into statements of deception—a clever way of trying to back out of the responsibilities of life. We as Christians must not condone anyone who is being led by their feelings to not do the things that they know are right.

So when you pick up in your spirit that someone is expressing how they feel to you for the wrong reason, this is how you should respond. We will use the same statements.

When he or she says, "I don't feel like going to work today; I wish I could just stay in bed," **you say, "I wish I could stay in bed, too, but these bills have to be paid."**

When he or she says, "I don't want to go to school to get my education," **you say, I'm not always happy about it, either, but I have to get an education.** When they say, "I wish I could watch the game today instead of going to church,"

you say," I wish I could watch the game, too, but God is more important."

Take notice that you are not denying the way the person feels because you yourself know that you feel the same way sometimes, but you are denying the intent that could be behind the feelings that he or she is expressing.

So whenever you sense that someone is being foolish by expressing his or her desires to you for the wrong reason, simply remind the person, using the communication style demonstrated in the examples, that his or her feelings are not an excuse. It is okay to express feelings as long as a person doesn't express them with the intention of escaping responsibility.

Proverbs 23:9 Speak not in the ears of a fool: for he will despise the wisdom of thy words.

Chapter Three

It Ain't the First Time

The principle of "It ain't the first time" is for anyone who foolishly overreacts to problems or situations—for people who act as though what happens to them has never happened to them before. For example, when rejected, the foolish will always overreact, as if they have never experienced rejection before in their life.

These people don't understand that whatever happens to them has already happened to them, because rejection is rejection and acceptance is acceptance, whichever way it comes. Now let's talk about how to respond to rejection the right way. Let's say someone gets rejected for a loan he needed to start a business, and his circle of friends asks him about the loan, and he says to them,

"They turned me down for the loan," and his friends begin to act foolish about it with joking remarks, and he replies, **"Yeah, but I'll be okay. It's not end of the world, and I have been turned down before. I'll get a loan sooner or later."**

Now that's a good, positive response. The part I want you to focus on, however, is when he said, "I have been turned down before. He recognized that this wasn't the first time he was rejected, and since he accepted that, he was able to use it as a small outlet to release some of the pain of being rejected and also to stay in control of his emotions. It's that simple. The scriptures say, "A man gets joy by the answer of his mouth," which means that your response or your reaction is far more important than what happens to you. So whenever it's time to give a response to a foolish crowd or a foolish person, remember to let them know that the Bible is right: there is nothing new under the sun; therefore I will not overreact.

Proverbs 17:24 Wisdom is before him that hath understanding; but the eyes of a fool are in the ends of the earth.

Chapter Four

When Foolish People Pretend They Don't Know the Answer

A fool will sometimes act as though he doesn't know something in order to escape whatever he doesn't want to face up to or doesn't want somebody to be right about. This principle will help you to stand on what you know and not doubt yourself when a foolish person is acting like they do not know something that you are sure they know. It's all an attempt to throw you off balance, but you must keep your focus and convey to the foolish person that you are right. Because if you don't, you will begin to doubt yourself and become what a foolish person loves—a green and naive person—because you didn't trust yourself but rather chose to trust his dishonesty.

Now let me offer a scenario and show you how to respond when a foolish person is acting like he or she doesn't know something. Let's say you have started a new job, and you are trying to recall how to do a certain part of your job. You decide to ask a coworker whom you saw doing the same job a few minutes earlier, and he or she tells you, "I don't know."

Now what do you do? Do you give this foolish person the benefit of the doubt, or do you trust yourself? You trust yourself. Why? Because you just saw this person do what he or she is saying he doesn't know how to do; plus, the person has been on this job for a number of years. So why wouldn't he or she know? So what do you say to this dishonest, foolish person? **Well, when they tell you they don't know, you pretend like you agree with them by saying, yeah right!, this will throw them off balance, then follow up with the truth by saying to them, you do know how to do this certain job.. This sounds real simple, but this is exactly the way you respond to a foolish person who pretends that he or she doesn't know. After you tell the person that he or she does know, you can follow up with reasons why you know that he or she does know.**

There will be many situations where this principle will be very much needed. Because the last thing a foolish person wants to do is to be honest with a person who is right about something the fool doesn't want them to be right about. So remember to trust your common sense rather than a foolish person's lies.

Proverbs 17:21 He that begetteth a fool doeth it to his sorrow: and the father of fool hath no joy.

Chapter Five

When a Foolish Person Pretends He or She Can Judge Your Ability by Your Appearance

Has a foolish person ever made these kinds of remarks to you before: "You don't look very smart" or "Your brother doesn't dress like he is a preacher" or "Your dog looks like he is a killer" or "You look too nice to be a drill sergeant"? Chances are you have heard a lot of remarks like these before. When a foolish person makes remarks like these to you, he or she is judging your ability by your appearance. The foolish use this tactic to try to get you to doubt and second guess your abilities.

They want to destroy your confidence by causing you to look at your appearance rather than staying focused on the truth of your ability. If they can get you to look at yourself from the outside to determine what kind of gifts and talents you have, they will have accomplished their goal. That's why it is extremely important for you to be aware of what's going on in every conversation with a foolish person. If you aren't, they will cause you to feel the way they want you to feel, which is always less than who you are. Now let me show you how to respond to those statements so that you will know how to answer a foolish person when he or she pretends he can judge your abilities by your appearance.

When they say to you, "You don't look very smart," **you say, "Don't let the way I look fool you. I am very smart."**

When they say to you, "Your brother doesn't dress like a preacher, **you say, "Don't be fooled by his attire because he is truly a preacher."**

When they say to you, "Your dog looks like a killer, **you say, "Don't let his size and his visage fool you, because he's a very friendly dog."**

When they say to you, "You look too nice to be a drill sergeant," **you say,**

"Don't be fooled by my smile or my facial expression, because I am very firm when it's time to be firm."

This is the way you answer a foolish person who thinks he or she can judge your ability by your appearance. This communication style will convey to the person that you don't judge yourself by your appearance but always by the unfailing truth of your abilities.

Proverbs 18:2 A fool hath no delight in understanding, but that his heart may discover itself.

Chapter Six

When Foolish People Encourage You to Make Decisions That Are Not in Your Best Interest

This chapter is focused on friends and family, because they are the people with whom you will most often use this principle. Your friends and family are the people from whom you don't mind taking advice or receiving encouragement. Your friends and family are the people who should always have your best interests at heart, but the sad reality is that sometimes the people you care about the most will begin to act foolish and encourage you to make decisions that are not in your best interest. No matter how much you love them and no matter how much they love you, there are times when you must not go along with them in their foolish games and plans, because friends and family sometimes have different ways of encouraging themselves or making themselves feel better than you do.

Let's say, for example, that you are talking to a friend or a family member about some disappointing events in your life. In the past, this particular person always gave great advice or encouragement, but for whatever reason this time they begin to give you foolish suggestions like "Let's go to the bar and get wasted," or that you should lie about your coworker in order to get a promotion or flirt with other people in order to get your spouse's attention or cheat on your taxes so that you can get more money. None of these statements have your best interests at heart. So how do you respond or answer these negative suggestions? **Simply say to the person, "You shouldn't want me to do those foolish things."** This is a powerful way to answer them because it reminds them of how a true friend or family member is supposed to act, and this response should be repeated until your family member or friend gets the point.

....*Proverbs 17:28 Even a fool, when he holdeth his peace, is counted wise: and he that shutteth his lips is esteemed a man of understanding.*

Chapter Seven

When a Fool Pretends You Don't Have Enough Ability to Win

This chapter is important because it teaches you how to protect your awareness of your abilities. You and God are the only ones who truly know what level your abilities are. There are some foolish people, however, who will pretend they know, in hopes of getting you to underestimate or underrate yourself. These foolish people will never judge you fairly but will always undermine and underrate you because they want to feel and be superior to you. If they can cause you to think that you have less ability than you really have, they can celebrate themselves as being better than you are. So we must be wise enough to recognize this deception, which is revealed when a foolish person begins to flatter himself or herself by undermining your ability. The foolish person will pretend you don't have enough physical, mental, or spiritual ability to succeed in everyday life. When the foolish begin to speak and act and treat you as though you are handicapped, this is how you answer them tactfully. **"I am smart enough to do this on my own"** or **"I am strong enough to do [this or that] without your help"** or **" I am wise enough to recognize a lie when I hear one."** I could give you many more examples like these, but I think you, the reader, is wise enough to get the point. So, instead of going on and on, acting as though you are not wise enough to comprehend, I choose not to flatter myself by offering a hundred examples. I choose not to undermine your sense of your own abilities for my own selfish reasons, thereby making myself into a fool.

Proverbs 19:1 Better is the poor that walketh in his integrity, than he that is perverse in his lips, and is a fool.

Chapter Eight

When Foolish People Pretend
They Have a Reason to Do Wrong

Many foolish people think that they have some good reason to do wrong and if you ask them why, they will tell you the exact reasons, without any kind of shame or guilt, because they feel their reasons are good enough to justify their wrong. We as Christians know that there is never a good reason to do wrong, no matter how much sense it appears to make, for doing the right thing or the wrong thing has nothing to do with making sense or logic. It is our purpose to do right, whether it makes sense or not. When a bird flies, he is not flying because it makes sense; he is flying because that's his purpose, what he was designed to do.

We as Christians also have to obey our purpose rather than logic, because our purpose transcends logic, which means we don't need a reason to do right!

Foolish people think that they can only do right if someone is doing right by them, and if someone does wrong by them, they think that they have a reason to return the wrong. Again, it's not about logic but about purpose! God created us to do right, not wrong. This deception can be heard in a basic conversation. For example, let's say you are talking to one of your coworkers, and he tells you that someone lied about him to the boss, and he tells you that he is going to get that someone back by lying about him. What would you say? How would you respond? Would you agree with him in thinking that he now has a good reason to do wrong, or would you remind him that there is never a reason to do wrong?

If you are going to do the right thing, this is how you should respond: you should say to him, **"We both know that this person was wrong to lie about you, but that's not a reason for you to lie about him."** As simple as that response sounds, it is very profound, because you are telling the foolish the absolute truth—that there is no reason to do wrong no matter how people treat you. Whether or not he complies, the choice belongs to him, but at least you can walk away knowing that you did not condone the wrong way of thinking.

Proverbs 19: 10 Delight is not seemly for a fool; much less for a servant to have rule over princes.

Chapter Nine

When Foolish People Pretend
They Can Live Your Life Better Than You Can

This may seem strange and confusing to some people, because from a logical or physical point of view, the foolish cannot live your life better than you can. Why?

Because they cannot cohabit with you in your body even to get the opportunity.

But, from a mental and spiritual point of view, they can, if you are naive or lack awareness . Let me explain how the foolish use this deception to gain control over the lives of people who are not aware of what's going on.

When the foolish act as though they can live your life better than you can, they will say and do certain things to make you believe this to be true. One of the first things the foolish will do is tell you what they would have done or said if they were in your shoes. As if your way of expressing yourself, which is the point of being yourself, and also doing what you feel is best for you, are wrong. But if you have not sinned against God, you are free to be yourself. The foolish want to control your life by trying to get you to regret being yourself simply because you didn't do what they would have done in every situation—as if God wants everybody to act like them. This also represents a selfish foolish person who wants everything done his way—even your personality. Now let's look at how to break down this deception. When the foolish person comes to you with that speech about what he or she would have done in your shoes, with the intention of trying to make you regret doing those things that are the sum total of you being yourself, this is how you answer: "I hear what you are saying, **but you are not me, and I am not you.**" This simple and profound response will kill that ploy every time. Be a broken record if you have to (**"you are not me, and I am not you"**). This response will convince them of what they already know—that they cannot live your life better than you can. Why? Because they will never be you.

As long as that barrier is there, everything the foolish say to you regarding what they would have done is moot and irrelevant because they are not you and you are not them. They can only be the best they can be, and you can only be the best you can be. Every person has the freedom to live out his or her own individuality and desires.

Proverbs 20:3 It is an honour for a man to cease from strife: but every fool will be meddling.

Chapter Ten

When Foolish People Pretend They Can Find Something Good Before They Can Find Something Bad

The foolish want people to believe that they can find something good before or faster than they can find something bad. I know this may seem confusing, but the foolish want you to be green and naive like a child, not knowing all the sad things about the world, not knowing that because of sin we have to go through different pains and struggles in our lives, not knowing that it's not easy to find the perfect job and that it's not easy to find the perfect mate. To put it another way, it's easier to find a penny on the street than it is to find a dollar; it's easier to find an enemy than it is to find a true friend; it's easier to find a lie than it is to find the truth; it's easier to find rejection than it is to find acceptance. The foolish know that without divine intervention from God, the average person will have to go through many "no's" before they can find one "yes," but the foolish don't want good people to know this truth. They want people to stay blind because then they can treat the good person like a child; they can run games and schemes on the person without the individual even recognizing it, and they can take his or her possessions, confidence, and self-esteem. So when a foolish person comes to you with something unrealistic, hoping to con you out of something that belongs to you, this is how you answer them. **Say to them, "What are the odds of that happening?" or "The chances of this or that happening are slim to none" or "The likelihood of that is zero."** Otherwise, you are just like a child to them, and they will try to take advantage of you every chance they get. If you have read and understood this chapter, however, you don't have to worry about a foolish person taking advantage of you in this area anymore because, when you know better, you can't help but do better.

Chapter Eleven

When a Foolish Person Pretends That Your Sense of Self-Worth Is Based on Your Ability to Avoid Making Mistakes

This principle is about foolish people who want to get other people to throw away their confidence. They want to manipulate people into basing their confidence on their ability not to make mistakes. The foolish know that anybody who is human has made, and will make, mistakes.

But if they can get people to believe that their confidence is based on being perfect, rather than on simply doing their best, they know that it won't be long before a person has cast away his or her confidence.

Because without a doubt you are bound to make a mistake. So we must remember that our confidence should not be based on our being perfect, but on our believing the best and doing our best.

Because if we throw away our confidence, we have lost before we even got started. And that's the goal of the foolish: for a person to feel so depleted in his or her confidence that they won't have to worry about that person showing up for a job interview or showing up for a performance competition or even standing up for his or her rights.

Now let's talk about how to recognize and respond to this ploy. The first thing the foolish are going to do is to try to get you to doubt all the great things you believe about yourself. For example, if you verbally acknowledge that you are a good person and because you are human you make one tiny mistake, the first thing the foolish person will say to you is, "I thought you said that you are a good person."

The foolish thus pretend that being a good person is equivalent to being a perfect person, hoping that you will accept this false notion and stop thinking that you are a good person and throw away your confidence.

Let's take another example. Say that a person proclaims that he is a great basketball player and, again, because that person is human, he misses a shot. Here come the foolish, saying, "I thought you said you are a great player," selling the false notion that being a great player is just like saying, "I am a perfect player" who never makes mistakes or falls short.

Again, this is done with the hope that this person will stop thinking that he is a great player and be afraid even to come back to the basketball court. So how do we respond to the foolish when they start talking foolishly, saying to you, "I thought you said you were great?" or "I thought you said you are smart?" or "I thought you said you are a beast in this sport or that sport?" This is how you answer: **I don't always get it right" or "I don't always know what to say" or "I am not always on top of my game,"** etc. This is simple but profound, because what you are conveying to the foolish is the fact that you still believe that you are great and good at what you do or who you are, and that you refuse to throw away your confidence simply because you will never be perfect in what you do or who you are.

Proverbs 26:1 As snow in summer, and as rain in harvest, so honour is not seemly for a fool.

Chapter Twelve

When Foolish People Pretend the Ultimate Goal of Your Personal Choice Is to Get Their Cooperation

This is another principle that's important to learn because without this understanding you will have little fortitude to stand up and go forward with your desires and ambitions.

This deception of the foolish will cause you to have a childlike mentality because, just like a child, you will be afraid to go forward with your ideals or goals, or even to verbalize your opinion about someone or something. As we all know, children need people's support and approval, plus cooperation. Why?

Because they are not old enough or mature enough to make wise, wholesome decisions for themselves, so they need their parents' permission before they can carry out their personal goals. It is okay for children to be subject to their parents' approval, but it's not acceptable for adults to be subject to the approval or cooperation of other adults; as adults we ought to be wise enough to make and carry out our own decisions without checking to see if it's okay with someone else. There are some foolish people who would love to keep you in a childlike mentality, however, because it gives them a means of control over you, since in the face of their disapproval you would become timid and indecisive to the point where you would even begin to keep all your goals and ambitions to yourself until you feel you have the foolish person's approval and cooperation.

So how do you convey to the foolish that their approval of you or their cooperation with you is not your No. 1 goal—that, as a matter of fact, it's not a goal at all? This is how you answer. Let's say you were expressing some creative ideals on your job, and immediately a foolish person blurted out, "I don't like your ideals!" **This is what you say: "I wasn't asking anyone to like my ideals, I was simply telling everyone my ideals."** Or, suppose you tell a friend that you are getting married, and he or she tells you that you are making a big mistake, **this is what you say: "I appreciate your honesty, but I wasn't looking for your opinion. I just wanted you to know that I am getting married."**
Notice how it is being communicated to the person that his or her disapproval has absolutely no effect on your personal choice. Why? Because you are not a child.

Here is one more example. Suppose you tell one of your sports buddies that you are going to defeat him in the game today, and he tells you that's it's not going to be easy to defeat him, **this is how you answer: "I am not expecting it to be easy. I just wanted you to know that I am going to win today.** It's all about communicating to the other person that you are not depending on their cooperation, because if you did you would never go forward with your goals and dreams, and that's exactly what a foolish person wants—for you always to be dependent on somebody else's approval.

Proverbs 26:6 He that sendeth a message by the hand of a fool cutteth off the feet, and drinketh damage.

Chapter Thirteen

When Foolish People Pretend They Can Judge the Freedom of Your Free Will by Your Status

This deception of the foolish is the reason for a number of people not succeeding in life. This deception is designed to stop you from doing what you have every right to do. This deception is so powerful that it will cause you to defeat yourself. Why? Because the very thing you are free to do, and have the ability to do, you refuse to let yourself do. This is a powerful deception because it attacks your free will. It deceives a person into putting restrictions on something God said is free, which means you are free to do whatever you desire to do, be it good or bad (though we as Christians have chosen to do that which is good). God has placed no limit on our choices, but the foolish use this deception and say there is a limit and that limit is recognized as status. Do you have enough status to do what you desire to do or desire to say, because if you don't, you can't. This is the restriction the foolish desire to place on your free will.

This deception is a great detraction. Why? Because it causes people to lose sight of the freedom of their free will and think that they have to be worthy or deserving to do and think what they wish when in reality that's not true. God never said you have to be worthy or deserving to use your free will. Being worthy or deserving has absolutely nothing to do with free will. This is one of the reasons for low self-esteem; people who are blinded by this deception always compare their status, position, skill, and prestige with someone else's. Whoever has the most status gets the right to feel good about themselves and those with lesser status have the right only to feel bad about themselves. But people don't need high status to choose to feel good about themselves, and they don't need low status to choose to feel bad themselves.

Now let's apply this principle so you understand how to recognize and respond to this deception. Whenever a person tries to go forward to think, say, or do something that's greater than their status or position, the first thing a foolish person will try to do is challenge that individual. Why? Because according to the foolish, this person is breaking a law that states that an individual can only think, say, or do something that's equal to their status or position in life. This is what the foolish will say to you to remind you that you are breaking a law that's made up by them: "Who do you think you are?" or "What do you think you are doing?" or "You aren't anybody important" or "Who are you to do this or say that?" or "You are not important enough to say this or say that."

And if a person is blind to this deception, he or she will succumb to this ploy and begin to feel exactly the way the foolish person wants the individual to feel—unworthy, not deserving enough to feel, do, or think the way anybody has the right to. That's why so many people have a dog-eat-dog mentality when it comes to gaining status, position, and prestige; they truly believe it will give them the right to feel good about themselves and the right to look down on somebody else. But this is how you answer the foolish when they make those kinds of statements: **"It doesn't matter who I think I am"** or **"Who I think I am is not important"** or **"It isn't about who I think I am"** or **"Whether I am this or that does not matter."** Why? **"Because in the end, I still can do and say what I want to."** Why? **"Because using my free will has absolutely nothing to do with how much status I have!"**

Proverbs 24:7 Wisdom is too high for a fool: he openeth not his mouth in the gate.

Proverbs 26:8 As he that bindeth a stone in a sling, so is he that giveth honour to a fool.

Chapter Fourteen

When a Foolish Person Pretends They Can Convince You of a Lie with a Deceptive Action

Understanding this principle will help you make better decisions in life; it will help you to be more patient, which is one of the key ingredients in making good decisions. It will stop you from jumping to conclusions about whatever you think you're so sure about. It will help you not be so judgmental toward your brothers and sisters; it will help you to be calm in the face of false accusations; and ultimately it will take you to a new level of insight that will enable you to distinguish the truth from a lie, which can be very hard to do whenever the truth looks just like a lie or a lie looks just like the truth. This is where the deception begins.

This is what the foolish use to deceive many people. Why? Because they tend to make their decisions based on how real something looks or sounds, which can fool you if you don't take the time to investigate the hidden difference between the truth and a lie. Sometimes they look alike, but as with identical twins there is always a slight difference; you must, however, get close enough to discover it. A person who doesn't understand this principle is defenseless against a foolish person who is accusing him of something that's not true, because if you are not aware of what a deceptive action is, you will have no defense against a false accusation. Wisdom is a defense to those who understand, but without the awareness you are blind. Because the false accusation from the foolish can look so real sometimes that if you weren't the one being accused, you, too, would believe it.

Now let me show you how to disarm the foolish false accusation. The first thing you do is reject the false accusation by saying to the foolish: **"That's not true."** Simple but powerful. Next, you simply begin to agree with the deceptive action by saying it this way: **"I know how it sounds"** or **"I know how it looks"** or **"I know how I said it"** or **"I know how I did it"** or **"The way I did things can cause you to think that way, but it's not true."** That's the way you disarm a false accusation from a foolish person.

Proverbs 26:10 The great God that formed all things both rewardeth the fool, and the transgressors.

Chapter Fifteen

When Foolish People Pretend They Can Criticize You for Going the Extra Mile to Reach Your Goal

This chapter will help you be successful in reaching your goals and dreams. Most goals and dreams are not reached because people never come out of their comfort zone to reach them. Some of these people really want to, but they are bound by deception and blind spots that hold them back with a paralyzing fear. People who suffer from this deception are afraid to let people know how excited they are about their dreams and goals. Most of the time these people are highly skilled and could easily accomplish their goals, but they have an irrational fear of the foolish people's judgment. They fear what the foolish might say if they go out of their way to reach their goals and dreams.

They are afraid that the foolish will ridicule them and say that what they are trying to accomplish isn't worth going out of your way for. This is a deception that the foolish use to try to take away the motivation from people who are trying to reach their goals.

Now let's deal with this deception. In order to not give in to this deception you must understand one fact: what you desire and care about the most may not be what somebody else desires or cares about. That said, how can a foolish person criticize or ridicule you for going the extra mile? They can't! Why? Because they don't feel as you do. If they felt the way you do about reaching your goals and dreams, they would do the very thing for which they unjustly criticize you, which makes them a hypocrite.

This is how you answer the foolish in this area. When they criticize or ridicule you simply because you are going the extra mile or miles to accomplish your dreams and goals, this is what you say to the foolish: **"If you felt the way I feel about what I am trying to do, you would do the same thing"** or **"If you liked what I like as much as I do, you would invest your time and effort in attaining it, too."** Answering the foolish this way will convey to them that you know too much truth to fall for that lie.

Proverbs 26:11 As a dog returneth to his vomit, so a fool returneth to his folly.

Chapter Sixteen

When a Fool Pretends You Should Change Everything about You That Doesn't Meet Their Expectations . . .

This chapter will help you to be proud of yourself . This chapter will help you to stay true to yourself and not be pressured to pattern yourself after foolish people. There are some things about all of us that make us different and unique. Most people don't mind being different and unique because being different and unique is how they express themselves and enjoy themselves. Unfortunately most people can only be who they are when they are far away from everybody else. Why? Because there are foolish people in every circle of life who have only one goal in mind and that is to get good people to stop being true to themselves and to follow the crowd or run the risk of being a loser and a nobody in their eyes.

If being yourself does not break one of God's commandments, you are free to be yourself, because if God wanted everybody to be the same, he would have made everybody the same. But if you are not strong in who you are and don't understand that you don't have to apologize for who you are, a foolish person can cause you to hate yourself, dislike yourself, regret being yourself around them and ultimately apologize to them for not being more like them, and this is the reason that some people are quiet and shy—not because they want to be, but because they feel like they have to be. Why? Simply because they are afraid of how a foolish person might see them or judge them.

So now let me explain how to answer a fool in this deception. The purpose of this deception is to cause you to be ashamed of everything that concerns you—your mistakes; your failures; your circumstances, gifts, and talents; your race; your gender; your personality; your success—anything that's a part of who you are. So when they bring up things about you that are unsuccessful in their eyes, hoping that you will feel embarrassed about the reality of who you are or what you are or where you are in life, you say to them: **"I am who I am" or "It is what it is" or "I can do what I can do" or "It's going to be what it's going to be" or "It was what it was."** When you respond like this, you are conveying to the foolish that you accept everything about yourself, whether they accept it or not, and you refuse to be ashamed of all the things they consider to be unsuccessful in your life.

Proverbs 26:12 Seest thou a man wise in his own conceit? There is more hope of a fool than of him.

Chapter Seventeen

When Foolish People Pretend Their Respect or Good Will toward You Is the Source of Your Future Success

This chapter will teach you how to be bold and independent of anybody who is foolish. There are some foolish people in every circle of life who want you to believe that your success in the future depends on you having their respect and good will toward you. Many people fall for this deception every day! They have foolish friends and foolish coworkers and family members who have convinced them that somehow their success is tied up in always keeping a foolish crowd happy. They believe that they have to laugh when it's not funny, say "yes" when they really mean "no," scratch where they don't itch, and stay late when they want to leave early. Why? Because some foolish people in every circle of life who have a certain amount of influence demand that anyone whom they outrank consider them as a god over their life. They want you to feel like you need them in order to go forward and be successful, and in some cases you do, but if you have to do foolish things for a foolish boss or foolish leader, it's not worth you being successful. Why? Because your integrity and your moral convictions are far more important, and besides, they are not the source of your past, present, or future success. Your source is the same one who wakes you up every morning—God, Jesus Christ; he is the one who works through anybody to make you successful whether they are foolish or not, and this truth, once recognized, must be communicated to foolish people who want you to believe that they are your source. So when they come to you with threatening implications in their conversation that they are not going to use their influence to help you be successful in the future if you don't dance to their music or give in to their foolish ways and agendas, **you say to them: "You are not my source" or "This job is not my source" or "Your good will toward me is not my source; nothing is my source but the Lord almighty God."**

These responses are very bold and direct, but this deception is also very bold and direct.

This will convey to the foolish leaders and bosses that you don't care who they think they are, because you know who they are, and you refuse to compromise your conviction for foolish people who want to believe that they are gods in your life.

Proverbs 27:22 Though thou shouldest bray a fool in mortar among wheat with a pestle, yet will not his foolishness depart from him.

Chapter Eighteen

When a Foolish Person Pretends He or She Can Dishonor Who You Are by Having the Wrong Interpretation of Your Action

This chapter will show you how to respond properly to foolish people who intentionally misinterpret your good action as a negative action so that they can cause others to speak ill of your good works. They want to downplay everything about you that's positive in order to create the type of image or reputation they want you to have. They want to distort and twist every action you take into something that will cause you to look bad. They don't want people to credit you with being a good person. Why? Simply because they want everybody to be foolish like them. Why? Because all foolish people need a crowd to entertain, so good, positive people are always a threat to foolish people.

Let's talk about how to recognize this deception and properly respond to it. The first step in recognizing this deception is to understand that the foolish are always looking for an opportunity to make you look bad. In this deception the foolish sit back and watch your actions to see which one can be distorted, and when they think they have found an action that can be intentionally misinterpreted, they will bring it to you and everybody else, accusing you of doing something wrong. This is how they will usually say it: "I saw you doing this negative thing" or "I saw you doing that bad thing" or "I saw you going to this bad place." When you hear false accusation against you in that kind of verbal format, this is how you answer the foolish. First, you disagree with it; second, you begin to tell the truth of what they really saw: **"What you saw me doing was this and not that"** or **"Where you saw me going was over here and not over there"** or **"How you saw me acting was good and not negative."** This is how you stop a foolish person from distorting your actions and causing others to speak ill of your good works.

Proverbs 28:26 He that trusteth in his own heart is a fool : but whoso walketh wisely, he shall be delivered.

Chapter Nineteen

When a Fool Pretends to Know the Truth of Your Situation So He or She Won't Have to Ask

This chapter will teach you how to correct a foolish person when he or she intentionally assumes the wrong things about you. Foolish people love to assume but hate to investigate. Why? Because they have already made up their mind about how they want to perceive you, and that's always in a negative light. Giving you the benefit of the doubt is always out of the question. Why? Because they don't care about what's right; they only care about implementing more foolishness, and this is another deception to help them reach their goal. This deception is used to give them a way out when people challenge them on their foolish assumptions and they are found guilty of intentionally assuming the wrong thing about you. Foolish people never want to own up to being wrong, but when it's clear that they were wrong, they will begin to try to cover themselves by using phrases like these: "I thought you were this negative thing or that negative thing" or "I didn't think you wanted this or that" or "I thought you were this kind of person or that kind of person," thinking that they can be excused because they accidentally thought the wrong things about you. But they can't be excused. Why? Because they didn't have to assume. They could have asked you or tried to get to know you as a person so that they could know the truth about you. But they don't care about the truth; they only care about spreading lies and nasty rumors about people. And this is why we have to hold the foolish accountable. When the foolish try to excuse themselves by telling you what they thought or what they think concerning you, this is how you answer: **"You thought, don't think you have to know" or "You think, don't think ask."** When you answer the foolish like this, you are conveying to them that they don't have any excuse for not knowing the truth about you or your situation, which will expose them for who they really are.

Proverbs 29:11 A fool uttereth all his mind: but a wise man keepeth it in till afterwards.

Chapter Twenty

When a Foolish Person Pretends That What They Believe Determines What I Believe

This chapter will help you to learn how not to expect the worst. It will change you from being pessimistic to being someone who is not afraid to want the best and expect the best, because God didn't give us the spirit of fear but the power of love and a sound mind. But there are a lot of foolish people in this world who want to see people live in fear. Why? Because they are living in fear.

Foolish people are always walking in doubt and unbelief. The greatest fools have said in their hearts that there is no God. Why? So that they can be free to live as they want to live, which, most of the time, is foolishly. The foolish don't want people to walk in positive faith, expecting the best, so they try to deceive you into believing what they believe. If they succeed, then you will be tormented by fear just as they are tormented by fear, expecting the worst.

Let's talk about how this deception works. When a foolish person sees you step out on faith to do something that they are afraid to do themselves, he or she will begin the deception by reminding you of all the bad things that could happen or go wrong, hoping that you will change your belief from expecting the best into expecting the worst. If you don't have a wall of wisdom up in your mind to ward off the doubt and unbelief, you will begin to buy into these things. So how do you respond to the foolish person? When they tell you all the bad stuff that could happen, you tell them: **"I am not hoping or believing that those bad things will happen"** or **"I am not expecting anything bad to happen"** or **"I am praying for the best to happen, not the worst."** Notice how this response conveys to the foolish that you will not allow them to impose their doubt and unbelief upon you, because you are wise enough to recognize that whatever a person believes the most will eventually come to pass, whether it is good or bad. So why would anyone expect the worst?

Proverbs 29:20 Seest thou a man that is hasty in his words? There is more hope of a fool than of him.

Chapter Twenty-One

When a Fool Pretends We Can Choose Good without Choosing Bad

This chapter will help you accept every part of reality. It will help you to take the good with the bad, and it will teach you to respect the fact that sometimes there is no gain without going through some pain. This is a reality that must be accepted in life in order to go forward with some of the goals and plans we have. You will learn how not to allow a foolish person to deceive you into depriving yourself of striving for the things you love simply because some of the things you love come with a price. But some people struggle with this truth. They don't fully accept this truth in their hearts, probably because they have been brainwashed by foolish people who have somehow taught them to be ashamed of accepting those things that are good but that can only be attained if we accept the bad that comes along with them. You might, for example, finally find the job of your dreams, but you have to relocate and move away from the people you love, or you have just bought the perfect house, but you are surrounded by unfriendly neighbors. The foolish want people to reject the truth of this reality; they only want you to accept those things that cost you nothing. Why? Because those things really don't make you happy, and that's the No. 1 focus of a foolish person—seeing you unhappy.

Let's discuss how to answer the foolish in this deception. When the foolish see you accepting those things that you love but that come with a price, they will begin to highlight all the bad things about your decision as if you don't already recognize them, hoping that you will feel you made a mistake.

This is how you answer them. **You say to them: "This or that bad thing comes with the territory" or "This or that struggle comes along with the job" or "Good times and bad times come along with living."** This response will convey to them that you don't look at the bad that comes along with your decision as abnormal but rather as a part of life that you have no problem accepting in order to have those things that you care about the most.

Proverbs 30:22 For a servant when he reigneth;
and a fool when he is filled with meat;

Chapter Twenty-Two

When a Fool Pretends You Are Not Smart Enough to Choose Your Own Goals and Preferences

This is another deception that a fool will try to use to control people. Because a fool loves to take advantage of your weaknesses and your blind spots. The foolish are always looking for the next person they can use like a puppet. In this deception the foolish try to undermine your intelligence. They want you to believe that you are not smart enough to choose your own goals or your own preferences, as if they are the ones who know what's best for you. Believe it or not, there are some people who are uncomfortable with making decisions for themselves. Why? Because they feel like their decisions have to please everybody else, and as a result they become indecisive people who always believe that what other people decide for themselves is far better than what they can decide for themselves. This is exactly the kind of person a fool wants you to be—someone who doesn't have a mind of his or her own. Nobody wants to be a people pleaser, no one wants foolish people to have control over them, but without knowledge of how to recognize the deception and how to respond to the deception, you will center your life around foolish people.

Let's talk about how to recognize and respond to this deception. When they come to you acting as though you are a child who does not really know what's best for you, undermining your intelligence and your love for yourself, this is the point at which you should recognize that the deception has started. Now that we recognize it, let's respond to it. When they pretend that you are not smart enough to choose your own goals and preferences, this is what you say to them: **"I know what I want" or "I know what I want to do" or "I know what I like" or "I know what I want to believe."** This may sound simple, but it's saying a lot because it's letting the foolish know that you will decide what is a wise choice for you, not them. You are also conveying to them that it's not about what everybody thinks you should do but rather what you want to do, so that no one can use their own logic to control the route or the direction of your life, because no one has that right but God.

Ecclesiastes 2:14 The wise man's eyes are in his head; but the fool walketh in darkness.

Chapter Twenty-Three

When a Fool Pretends You Have to Have Good or Bad Action in Order to Have Good or Bad Character

This chapter will help you have a greater understanding of how far a fool will go to try to deceive you, because a fool is a great pretender. A fool is a great actor, and he will play any role that will make him successful in winning good people's hearts and trust. Why? Because a fool is not happy until he has caused someone to be deceived.

This deception is designed to take advantage of all the people who are not wise enough to understand that any action, whether good or bad, is not necessarily a reflection of someone's heart; it can be a ploy. It can be a foolish person's attempt to gain access to your heart. Some people are naive enough to look only at what people are doing, rather than looking at why they are doing what they are doing. This is the first test that must be passed—not allowing a person's action to be the first and final step in proving their authenticity. Otherwise, you will be the victim of foolish people's deceptions. In this deception the foolish want you to think that they are good people and that they are on your side, simply because they have taken a series of good actions, but again, good action is not the final test. Remember, the final test is why they are doing what they are doing.

But how do you know when their motives are wrong? Simply by being patient, because patience is a tool that can eventually expose all foolish people's deceptions. When you discover that their motives are wrong yet the foolish want you to act as though they are good, loving people because they have taken a series of good actions, this is how you respond to them: **"You don't have to be a good person to perform some good action"** and **"You don't have to be a bad person to perform some bad action."** This is a powerful response. Why? Because you are conveying to the foolish that their good action can never disguise their foolish hearts.

Ecclesiastes 4:5 The fool foldeth his hands together, and eateth his own flesh.

Chapter Twenty-Four

When a Fool Pretends That the Bigger Your Problem Gets, the Less God Can Do about It

In this chapter you will learn how to keep trusting God no matter what. Many people trust God on the front end when things are looking slightly bad, but as things go from bad to worse, their faith begins to shrink. They begin to walk in doubt and unbelief, and they begin to think that the problem has become too large for God almighty to solve. This is one of the main reasons people throw in the towel—because unconsciously they have made their problem bigger than their God, which gives a foolish person another blind spot to take advantage of. That's why it is important for believers to truly know what it means to be God. The most simple and profound definition of God is that he is all power; there is absolutely nothing outside his control. This must be clearly seen and accepted in every inch of your heart so that you won't allow the foolish to discourage you from trusting God. The way they will try to accomplish that is simply to observe your life, and the moment they see something in your life go from bad to worse they will begin to highlight it by making comments like these: "Gosh, your situation is getting worse" or "Your problem is getting bigger" or "Your dilemma has gotten out of control," hoping that they can cause you to think that your problem has gone too far even for God to solve, because they know that you will then surely throw in the towel.

But we must communicate to the foolish what we understand about God, which is this: God is all power. It therefore makes no difference how bad our problem or dilemma gets, even if our situation comes to the point of death. Why? Because God is all power! So when the foolish come to you trying to get you to throw in the towel because your problem is getting bigger, **this is how you answer them: "It doesn't matter how bad it gets; God is still able" or "It doesn't matter how long it's been; God can still do it" or "It doesn't matter how defeated my situation looks; God can still give me the victory."** When you answer like this, you are conveying to the foolish that, no matter how large your problems become, they will never be larger than the one who can calm any storm, the Lord almighty God.

Ecclesiastes 7:6 For as the crackling of thorns under a pot, so is the laughter of the fool :this also is vanity.

Chapter Twenty-Five

When a Fool Pretends He or She Can Cause You to Overreact by Selling You an Obvious Lie

In this chapter you are going to learn how to stay calm whenever a foolish person tries to cause you to overreact with an obvious lie. The foolish use obvious lies to try to gauge how wise you are in order to see whether or not they can make a fool out of you. The foolish want to see you acting as though what they are saying to you is really true, which will surely cause you to look unwise and greener than grass in July, but we are not going to let that happen. Why? Because in this chapter you are going to learn how to recognize this deception and also how to respond to it.

This deception is recognized by calculating the true probability of what a foolish person is saying to you and finding out how far from the truth are the lies they are trying to sell you. Then you must know how to answer them; knowing how to answer a fool is very important. This response is going to be very unusual, but it will convey to the foolish what needs to be conveyed and that is that you are not unwise or greener than a John Deere lawnmower. So now allow me to give you an example. Let's say you work at a delivery company and a foolish person says to you that this Friday is the Friday that all delivery companies gives away free products. This is an obvious lie, right?

It's so obvious that you must go along with it in conversation—certainly not in your actions—because this will cause their deception to backfire on them, making them look more foolish than they already are. **So say to the foolish: "You are right. Go get your car, and I will load up your trunk for you.** Now this response will profoundly convey to the foolish that you are so far from falling for an obvious lie that you would even go along with an obvious lie in conversation but that you will never go along with it in your actions, so the joke and the shame are on them.

Ecclesiastes 10:3 Yea also, when he that is a fool walketh by the way, his wisdom faileth him, and he saith to every one that he is a fool.

Chapter Twenty-Six

When a Foolish Person Pretends You Don't Have the Right to Be Proud of Yourself If You Had to Get Some Help to Win

In this chapter you are going to learn how not to be ashamed to ask for help, to make certain that you accomplish your goals. You will learn how not to allow foolish people to make you regret receiving help from people who want to see you succeed. One of the most important goals of the foolish is to see you fail, and this is why they try so hard to brainwash you out of accepting help: they know that the more help you receive, the more likely it is that you will succeed. There are some people who are too proud to ask for help, because they feel that if someone has to help them, their victory is somehow watered down.

That's not true, however; it is only a deception, because receiving help is a reflection of a person's determination to win.

Now let's talk about how to respond to this deception when a foolish person comes to you with it. When a foolish person sees you winning in something, he or she will immediately try to find out whether or not you received any help. If you did, the person will ask you, "What are you rejoicing for? Someone had to help you win." Notice how that comment implies that you shouldn't be rejoicing or happy over your victory. This is how you answer the foolish person to let him or her know that you don't have any shame or regret about having received help in order to succeed. **Say to the person: "I sure did receive some help" or "That's right. I got some help."** This is a great answer, because it is not what the foolish individual is expecting to hear from you. The foolish do not expect you to own up to the truth.

They expected you to stop rejoicing and being happy over your victory.

They thought that they could cause you to look at receiving help from a foolish, prideful, and wrong perspective, but they were wrong, because as long as you didn't cheat, you have every right to be excited about winning, even if you had to get some help from other people to do it.

Ecclesiastes 10:12 The words of a wise man's mouth are gracious; but the lips of a fool will swallow up himself.

Chapter Twenty-Seven

When a Fool Pretends He or She Can Downgrade Your Action to Nothing

This is another chapter that will help you to be strong and firm in the things that you are proud of, because there are many deceptions that a fool will try to use to make you minimize or disown the things you love. Everything about you and everything that concerns you, whether big or small, is only as important as you want it to be. We all have the right to value what we want to value without anyone else's permission or approval, but the foolish want people to believe that they can only be proud of the things that are popular and exciting to everyone—as if the value of the things you like is based on how many other folks consider it as likable, too. They would have you believe that if you are the only one who likes what you like and does what you do, it is worthless. It is sad that some people buy into this false notion and learn only to show excitement for the things they love when they are all alone. They feel that when they are alone they are free from the judgment of foolish people, but that's not true freedom; it's bondage. True freedom is being able to show your excitement for all the small things you love in the midst of a foolish crowd.

Foolish people want you to conceal the things that they consider to be insignificant when they come around. For example, let's say you are on your lunch break at work, watching a TV show that you like to watch. It's really not a popular show, and most people consider it boring, but you find it exciting. Suddenly a foolish coworker comes into the break room and asks what you are watching. Since you know it is an unpopular show that most people consider boring, you answer the foolish coworker out of fear by saying, "Nothing. Just some old show." Notice how you minimize your excitement all the way to nothing; you told your foolish coworker that you were watching "nothing." Why? Because you were ashamed of being excited about something that most folks consider to be worthless. So what is the correct way of responding to this foolish coworker? The correct way is to be honest and not conceal your excitement. **Say to the foolish coworker, "I am watching one of my favorite shows,"** and this straightforward, honest answer will convey to the foolish that you are not ashamed or embarrassed to show your excitement about anything that you love. It will show that you understand that what you choose to be excited about doesn't have to be popular with anyone but you.

Ecclesiastes 10:14 A fool also is full of words: a man cannot tell what shall be; and what shall be after him, who can tell him?

Chapter Twenty-Eight

When Fools Underestimate Your Ability Because of Their Own Doubt and Unbelief

This chapter will teach you how not to be fazed or disturbed by foolish people's doubt and unbelief. Because foolish people are full of doubt and unbelief, they don't think they can act any other way than foolishly. But they are not girded up with the truth; they are girded up with trickery, lies, and deception. They are always trying to gain control over your life, hoping to shape you into a mental slave. This is what the foolish desire, and for every foolish desire that they have, they have deceptive ways to bring it about.

In this deception, the foolish will intentionally doubt and underestimate your skills, mainly because you have, for your own personal reasons, chosen not to use or display your skills and abilities. They think that by doubting and underestimating you and telling you what you can't do or what they don't believe about you, they will somehow cause you to want to prove yourself to them so badly that you will suspend your reasons and begin to display your skills and talents. But you must not allow them to provoke you into proving yourself, because if you do, they are controlling you, and that's exactly what the foolish want. This is a sneaky way of causing you to relinquish your control into their hands, but there is a way to respond to this foolish deception without being pressured into proving yourself. When the foolish intentionally underestimate you with doubt and unbelief, the correct way of responding is to suggest that they do what they should be doing—believing and trusting. When, for example, the foolish begin to doubt you intentionally by telling you what you cannot do, **this is how you should answer them: "Trust me; I can do this or that, if I want to" or "Believe me, if I wanted to do this or that, I definitely could do it."** This is a powerful response because you are conveying to the foolish that you are 100 percent sure about your skills and abilities and that at any time you can use your skills and abilities.

Proverbs 12:16 A fool's wrath is presently known: but a prudent man covereth shame

Chapter Twenty-Nine

When a Fool Pretends You Are Using Your Gifts and Talents to Calculate Your Success

In this chapter you will learn how to disconnect yourself from a foolish person's judgment. You will also learn how to perform and speak in front of a foolish crowd without having any unconscious thoughts on whether or not good people or foolish people are accepting you. You will learn how to go forward with all your endeavors without having any fear or hesitation. You are going to be powerful in whatever you are doing, because your motives are going to be pure, and whenever you have pure motives, there is no more fear. Why? Because your focus is on the Lord, rather than on the calculation of your success.

Let me explain what I am talking about. When calculating success, a person unconsciously gauges how many people are going to like or dislike what he or she is about to do or perform, making the opinions of both good people and foolish people into a false god. If people calculate that most others are going to like what they are about to do, they will be confident. If they calculate the opposite, they will be nervous and fearful, both before and doing the performance.

This is a deception that will destroy your focus, causing you to follow a foolish crowd rather than your own conviction. If you are a victim of this deception, your life and your God-given dreams are being neglected. How? Because you have been brainwashed into believing that being accepted by good people and foolish people is far more important than carrying out your own convictions. People who are blinded by this deception will always gravitate toward those systems, styles, and formats that are already accepted. They will eventually stop using their own creativity and become very indecisive. Why? Because they will be spending too much time trying to calculate what will or will not be accepted by the foolish crowd.

Now let's get into the application of this deception and learn how to recognize and respond to the foolish people who try to implement it. The way to recognize this deception is first to be true to God and yourself by performing and verbalizing everything that is in your heart to accomplish. If your performance or your conversation is not accepted or popular in other people's eyes—mainly the foolish people's eyes—the foolish will always let you know. They will give you disapproving looks or make negative remarks or they will ignore your performance altogether. Finally they will step up to you and verbalize the thoughts of all the people who didn't approve of or like your performance or conversation, hoping to cause you to reject and regret your performance or conversation.

This is how you answer the foolish. You simply say to them: **"I didn't do my performance to see how many people were going to like it"** or **"I didn't say what I said to see whether or not you were going to agree with it"** or **"I am not doing what I am doing to see how many people I can get to join me,"** etc. These responses will convey to the foolish that you are not doing what you do for the praise and acceptance of people, but for the glory of God.

Proverbs 18:6 A fool's lips enter into contention, and his mouth calleth for strokes.

Chapter Thirty

When the Foolish Pretend That High Status and Position Give Them the Right to Bend the Rules

This chapter will focus on holding everybody—including the foolish people, or especially the foolish people—accountable for doing what is right.

Why? Because foolish people are the ones who think they are above the law or the rules simply because their status and position may be greater than everyone else's. Not only are they deceiving themselves by embracing this false notion, but they are also trying to deceive everyone else. Why? Because if they have to obey the rules just like people with low status and low position, they want to have a reason to feel superior to those people. Why? Because we will all be held accountable to the same rules and regulations, and no one will be greater than anyone else, but the foolish can't be happy with this arrangement. They have to convince themselves that whoever has the most status and position deserves to do wrong without having to pay the price. This kind of foolishness is going on all around us—on our jobs; in our schools, our homes, and churches; in the entertainment industry; and in politics. Why?

Because a lot of folks don't know how to respond to this kind of deception.

There is a precise and effective way of responding to this deception. First, this deception must be recognized, which is simple. When foolish people are in your circle of life, and they begin to break rules and do wrong, thinking that you are not allowed to confront them or admonish them about it, this is the point at which you must deal with this deception. First, confront them about breaking the rules. Second, brace yourself for their reaction, which will be the foolish firmly and angrily reminding you who they are and how great their status and position are. They are going to remind you in a threatening and arrogant way, hoping that this attitude will intimidate you and dissuade you from confronting them about their wrongdoing. This is how you answer the foolish when they attempt to remind you of who they are. You simply remind them that people with high status and position must do the right things and abide by the law like everyone else. Use their title and status to address them. **Say to them, for example, "The preacher must do right, too," or "The police must do right, too," or "The politician must do right, too," etc.** Whatever great status or position they have, that's what you use to remind them and answer them with.

This will convey to the foolish in a profound way that no matter how great their status or position or power, they will still be held accountable, just like everyone else.

Proverbs 18:7 A fool's mouth is his destruction, and his lips are the snare of his soul.

Chapter Thirty-One

When a Fool Pretends There Is Only One Way of Winning

The foolish want people to believe that there is only one way of winning for many reasons. If they can get you to buy this foolish lie, they will put you in a position where you blindly believe that there is no other way of winning or being successful, which will cause you to be unsuccessful in many areas in your life. Why? Because you have been fooled into to not asking or seeking help from folks who would love to help you. The foolish want you to think, arrogantly, that you don't need anyone, because you are totally self-reliant and self-sufficient.

They want you to be a one-person army or a one-person gang, when it's clear and known to everyone that you need some help. As the saying goes, there is more than one way to catch a fish: you can use a net, a fishing pole, or a spear, like some folks in far-away countries and remote places. You can even pay somebody to catch some fish for you. There are many ways to get a job done.

You would think that this truth would be embraced by everyone, but it's not. There are people who are blind and cannot see this obvious truth. All of us fail to know some things that we should know, and it's the job of foolish people to take advantage of what good people don't know. How do the foolish accomplish that? By observing your life, and when they see you struggling with your endeavors to the point of almost failing, they will begin to ridicule you with negative comments and predicting your defeat. Why? Because they know you are not going to ask for help, nor are you going to try new ways of reaching your goals, but when the foolish come to you as if you are blinded by this deception, show them that you are not. Let's say, for example, that you had a flat tire, and you tried to change it, but you could not, and your foolish coworkers immediately started to ridicule you as if you were not going to get your flat tire changed. **This is what you say to them: "I am not worried about it because I can call my mechanic or my brother or a friend or anybody else who would love to help me."** This is how you answer the foolish; you simply communicate to them that you have recognized all your options for winning and also that you are not so prideful that you would rather lose than look for help outside of yourself.

Proverbs 26:3 A whip for the horse, a bridle for the ass, and a rod for the fool's back.

Chapter Thirty-Two

When the Foolish Pretend They Can Neglect Their Responsibilities Because of Your Strong Points

In this chapter you are going to learn to recognize and respond to foolish people who want to use and abuse your gifts, your talent, and your good morals for their own benefit because the last thing foolish people want to do is to be responsible. They would rather take advantage of people who can't recognize that they are being exploited. There are people who are not wise enough to know that they are being used by foolish people.

So how do you recognize when a fool is trying to take advantage of you? Simply by being aware of your strong points and what you are responsible for. Just because you are highly gifted and talented and able to do everybody's job doesn't mean that you are responsible for doing everybody's job. And just because you are such a loving person that you always forgive doesn't mean that people don't have the responsibility to do right by you. Understanding this truth is the first step toward not allowing foolish people to take advantage of you.

Now the only thing left is to learn how to verbalize or communicate this to foolish people. So how do you do that? Let's say you have a foolish coworker who is much older than you are, who is always trying to get you to do most of the work because you are younger. What do you say to him? **This is what you say: "I am not going to let you abuse my youth."** Here is another example: let's say you are rich, and every time you and your friends go out to eat dinner, they always expect you to pay. Again, what do you say? This is what you say: **"Yes, I am rich, but I am not going to allow y'all to abuse the fact that I am rich."** Here is another example: let's say that everybody knows you to be a nice person, and some of your foolish associates try to take advantage of you by overstepping their boundaries, what do you say to them? **This is what you say: "I am a nice person, but I am not going to allow you to abuse my kindness."**

This is how you answer foolish people who think that they can take advantage of your strong points.

Proverbs 27:3 A stone is heavy, and the sand weighty; but a fool's wrath is heavier than them both.

Chapter Thirty-Three

When a Fool Pretends Your Reactions Can Only Be a Reflection of Your Successes or Failures

In this chapter you will learn how to give wise answers to foolish people who think they already know what kind of reaction you are going to have after success or failure. Your life is always put under a microscope by foolish people who want to read and understand you like a children's book, so that they can know exactly how to hurt you and deceive you with all their many games and deceptions.

The more we know, the less they can deceive us. When bad things happen to a person, or failure is the outcome of a person's efforts, a fool will take a front-row seat to witness that person falling apart with shame and embarrassment. The reason a fool is so confident that this will be the case is that so many people do. Somebody said, however, that it's not what happens to you that matters, but your reaction, which means your reaction doesn't have to be a reflection of your failures or the bad things that happen to you. If you know God, you know that all things are working together for your good, and for that reason alone, you can choose to have a positive, optimistic reaction. That will cause all foolish people to be baffled.

Now let's discuss how to convey this to foolish people. When foolish people witness a positive reaction when they thought for sure you would have a negative reaction, they will be so confused that they will come to you and ask, "Are you not going to get upset and fall apart about this?" and this is how you should answer: **"You would definitely think that I would, but I am not going to."** This response is simple but powerful. Why?

Because you are conveying to the foolish person that even though it is natural and normal for people to respond from a negative, discouraged standpoint, they don't have to; they can still have a great, positive attitude even after experiencing great disappointment and defeat.

*Proverbs 9:6 Forsake the foolish, and live;
and go in the way of understanding.*

Chapter Thirty-Four

When a Fool Pretends You Don't Have Any Physical Proof or Evidence That You Can Be a Winner

In this chapter you will learn how a foolish person will intentionally overlook your ability to win in a certain area of your life. You will also learn how the fool will act so surprised that you are succeeding in what you are doing, to somehow downplay your success and insinuate that you are just lucky, when all the time they know that you have the ability to win in that area. The goal is to rain on your parade and to get inside your head to distract you, because the foolish know there is nothing that they can do about your ability. If the fool can somehow cause you to overlook the proof of your ability, you will not have the confidence that it takes to be at your best, even though you have more than enough ability. Just think about some of the people you may know who have more than enough ability to win in a certain area of their lives, yet they lack the confidence to do so. Now this ploy that the fool uses to deceive you may seem harmless, but it's not—not when it can cause a person to miss out on what could be a lot of success in life.

Now let's see how this ploy works. For example, when a fool says in a surprised way, **"Wow, how did you win the game?"** your response should be, **"Well, as skilled as I am in this game, I better win at least most of the time."** Or the fool may say, **"Wow, I can't believe that you were not nervous speaking in front of all those people."** Your response should be, **"Well, with all the skill that I have in public speaking, I better not be afraid or nervous to do so."** Or let's say the fool says, **"Wow, I can't believe that you did not cheat me when you could have,"** your response should be, **"Well, as much as I value my integrity and fear God, I better not ever cheat you or anyone else."**

Those are some of the responses that the foolish need to hear. When they come at you with foolishness, you must come back at them with wisdom.

Proverbs 9:13 A foolish woman is clamorous: she is simple, and knoweth nothing.

Chapter Thirty-Five

When a Fool Pretends That Their Ideal about What Is Good or Bad Should Be Your Ideal As Well

Now here is another deception that the foolish use to mislead people every day: trying to get you to adopt their ideal about what is good or bad. As the Bible tells us, some people will call good, evil and evil, good. Isaiah 5:20 That's why you will learn in this chapter how to recognize this ploy and to disarm it so that you can avoid being a victim of this foolishness. Now the goal of the foolish with this deception is to cause you to question your ideals about what is good or bad, because the foolish want you to think that there are no absolutes with regard to good and bad. Based on the word of God, however, there *are* absolutes. The foolish also want you to question your personal preferences, your likes and dislikes. You see, the fool's whole plan is to control your thinking, but your thinking won't be controlled by a fool if you understand this principle.

So let's see how this ploy works. A fool will tell you, for example, that he had a good time by getting drunk at the club last night and that he wants you to come with him next time. **Your response should be, "Thanks for the invitation, but that's not what I call having a good time."** Or let's say your foolish boss tells you that, starting the following week, you will see a big raise on your check, but it turns out to be small. **Your response should be, "Sir, is this your idea of a big raise?"** Notice how you convey to him that you refuse to adopt his idea of a big raise. Or let's say you try to replace the fuel pump on your car, but it did not turn out right, and a foolish person asks you, "Why did you try to do it yourself anyway?" **Your response should be, "Well, I tried to save a lot of money just by doing it myself."** With that response, you convey to the fool that you are not ashamed to own your ideal, even though your attempt was not successful.

Those are a few responses that will help you to be wise when a fool comes at you with that kind of foolishness.

Proverbs 10:1 The proverbs of Solomon.
A wise son maketh a glad father: but a
foolish son is the heaviness of his mother.

Chapter Thirty-Six

When a Fool Pretends That a Small Issue Should Be the Main Issue

This deception is designed to cause you to overlook what's really important and to overfocus on what's not, because the fool knows that if you spend most of your time addressing the small matter, then there will hardly be any time left to deal with big and urgent matters. Some of the small issues that foolish people present to us are not even real issues at all, but just made-up issues, again designed to distract you from the true issue. Foolish people don't mind overlooking the real issue, because they feel their time is better spent when they can implement foolish ideals that will cause people to stumble in regard to the good that they may be trying to do.

So beware and understand that just about every time you attempt to do something that's good, there will be foolish people trying to come up with a ploy to stop you. But it's good to know that there are also people who, instead of spending their time trying to be a thorn in your flesh, will use their time to encourage and help you.

Now let's look at how foolish people implement this ploy; for example, a foolish person might suggest that you should miss church because you don't have a suit to wear. **Your response should be, "Well, it's not about whether or not you have a suit to wear to church; it's about having a desire to go to church in order to have fellowship with other believers and to worship God."** Notice how the foolish person tried to interfere with the main issue by presenting you with a small issue that really doesn't have to be an issue at all. Here is another example: let's say you see some shoes that you are about to buy, but a foolish person suggests that you should not buy the shoes, because they are not name brand shoes. **Your response should be, "Well to me, it is not just about whether or not the shoes are name brand; it's more about how they look and how they feel. That's what's important to me."**

So with these two examples you can see that, if you are not careful, you could miss out on some things that you want all because of foolishness.

Proverbs 10:14 Wise men lay up knowledge: but the mouth of the foolish is near destruction.

Chapter Thirty-Seven

Don't Blame Yourself for What You Don't Know

People who want to cope in life should know that this chapter will be a great help for them. There are many things we will not know simply because we are human, and people understand that fact. The foolish, however, will see that as an opportunity to exploit that part of your life and try to make you feel guilty for not knowing a certain thing. This will be a false guilt, but the door in your mind will be open for the foolish to lie to you by saying that there is something wrong with you. You will begin to feel as if you are not smart or competent, and at that point you will begin to blame yourself for what you don't know. You will start thinking that if you were smart and if there was nothing wrong with you, you would know the answer, when the only thing wrong is that the foolish pretend you are supposed to know everything.

We only know what we have been taught or what we have gleaned from experience. When the foolish person tries to insinuate that you are incompetent because of what you don't know, there is no reason to feel ashamed, because there is no difference between you and them in that aspect of life. You have to learn to convey that to them, and then they will know that this ploy does not work with you. Here is an example. Let's say you took a friend to see a movie, and you both agree that the movie was not good, don't say to your friend, "I shouldn't have brought you to see this movie," as if you are the one to blame for the movie not being good. This is what you should say:

"If I had known that this movie would turn out not to be good, I would not have brought you to see this movie." It is unfair to blame yourself for what you don't know; you can only blame yourself for the things you do know. For instance, if you knew the movie would not be a good movie and you took your friend anyway, then you are to blame, because you already knew. But if you don't know, it is not your fault, no matter how badly the foolish might want it to be.

Proverbs 14:1 Every wise woman buildeth her house: but the foolish plucketh it down with her hands.

Chapter Thirty-Eight

Making Sense for the Wrong Reason

This form of manipulation will deceive you in many different ways if you are not wise enough to read between the lines. Once the foolish know that you are blind in this area of your life, they will use this deception to get you to do what they want you to do. If you don't understand what is going on, you will quickly become a victim of this foolish deception. That it will make sense is at the root of this manipulation. The foolish want you to think that as long as it makes sense you are supposed to do it. If you understand that just making sense is not enough—that the other person also needs to have the right motives—you will not fall for this scheme, and that blind spot in your life will be gone. The bottom line to resisting this form of manipulation is not to focus so much on how much sense the foolish are making, but rather to focus on their motives. By doing that, you will be able to discern what to do and what not to do.

Let's say, for example, that you were at the store trying to buy the latest flat-screen TV, and it was the last one in stock, and another customer who was foolish wanted the same TV. They start making sense to you for the wrong reason by telling you that it would be much cheaper to get another brand that is also a flat-screen TV but a lot bigger. You know that their motives are wrong, so **this is what you say: "You have made a lot of sense and spoken the truth, but I know what I want."** This response is simple but powerful. Why? Because you recognized the deception and responded wisely to the foolish person behind the deception, and as a result you were able to keep your focus on buying exactly the kind of TV you wanted without being deceived or manipulated.

Proverbs 14:3 In the mouth of the foolish is a rod of pride: but the lips of the wise shall preserve them.

Chapter Thirty-Nine

Don't Blame Yourself for Things That Are Outside Your Control

There are many things outside our control in life, and if you don't understand this truth, you will automatically feel obligated to take the blame for things you can do nothing about. By taking the blame, you will feel guilty, as if you had done something wrong, when the only thing wrong is your inability to see and accept the truth. But if you embrace this truth, you will have more peace in your life and your worries and fears will decrease. Why? Because you will have the serenity to accept the things you cannot change. The only thing you *can* change is your own actions, which makes you responsible for your actions, but you have foolish people who want to make you responsible for their actions, which is a major deception and lie that they want you to buy. When you know and accept the truth, you won't be a victim of that lie, because you cannot be blamed for things outside your control, including foolish people's actions, but this must be conveyed to the foolish.

Here is an example. Let's say a foolish coworker wants to borrow some money from you, and he says, "If you don't let me borrow the money, the phone company will cut my phone off." See how he is trying to make you feel responsible for something outside your control? So how do you respond? **This is what you should say: "I understand, but that's not my problem."** Here is another example. Let's say a foolish person is trying to make you feel guilty because you make better grades than he does in school. This is how you should answer: **"I can't help that I make better grades than you do, and for that reason I will not feel guilty."**

Why? Because it is outside your control;
you can only be responsible for your own actions.

So this is the wise way to respond to foolish people who try to manipulate you into blaming yourself for things that are outside your control.

Proverbs 15:7 The lips of the wise disperse knowledge: but the heart of the foolish doeth not so.

Chapter Forty

When Foolish People Pretend You Will Choose Something "Worse" before You Will Choose Something "Bad"

Foolish people have many ploys that they use against us every day. Because some people cannot recognize these ploys, they become easy victims of foolish people's deception. That's why it is important to increase your awareness; so that you won't become a victim of deception. This ploy is designed to sway you to relegate

yourself to a lower position than you have to. It is designed to cause you to go from bad to worse, because sometimes in our lives we are faced with a bad or even a worse choice; nevertheless, a decision must be made. But that's when the foolish will try to sway you to feel indifferent about your dilemma, since these are both undesirable choices. If they sway you to choose "worse" over "bad," they have succeeded in their ploy. Let's say, for example, that you are having some financial problems, and one of your foolish cousins suggests that you sell some drugs. **This is how you should respond: "Before I ever choose to sell drugs, I will choose to get another job and take the slow route to get out**

of debt." Now this is a simple response, but a very powerful one. Why? Because it conveys to the foolish that just because you are faced with two undesirable choices, the best and wisest choice must still be made.

Proverbs 15:20 A wise son maketh a glad father: but a foolish man despiseth his mother.

Chapter Forty-One

When a Fool Pretends What You Have to Offer Is Not Worth Anything

This chapter will help you not to feel bad about yourself when a fool intentionally overlooks what you have to offer just because it's coming from you. This is a ploy to make you ashamed to the point that you would hide your gifts, ideas, and talents.

The root of this deception is for you to believe that what you have to offer is not worth anything. Some of the ways a fool will implement this lie are by brushing you off, ignoring you, and being indifferent toward you. If you are not aware of this lie, it will be an ongoing struggle for you to show what you have to offer, and you will live a life of quiet ambition. The foolish know they can't destroy what God has blessed you with, but if they can deceive you into not being excited about what you have to offer and just keeping it to yourself, then they have won. For example, let's say your company has a new position opening that pays more money and you apply for it,

but your foolish boss tells you that he is going to hire someone who you know is far less qualified than you. How do you respond? **This is what you say: "That's too bad for the company, sir,**

because I know I can do a better job." Here is another example. Let's say your foolish brother-in-law needs his car fixed, and you offer to fix it for free, but he declines because he doesn't think that much of you. How do you respond? **This is what you say: "That's too bad, because you could have had your car fixed for free."** This response will convey to the foolish that the joke is not on you but on them.

Proverbs 17:25 A foolish son is a grief to his father, and bitterness to her that bare him.

Chapter Forty-Two

When a Fool Pretends a Good or Bad Sign Doesn't Mean Anything

In this chapter you will see how foolish people will act as if the handwriting is not on the wall in order to deceive you, so you will think that things are fine when they are not or that things are bad when they are not. The fool's goal is to cause you to ignore all the red flags and the warning signs that will indicate what's really going on. The fool wants you to ignore the signs until his or her true agenda has been fulfilled. Once the fool's agenda has been fulfilled, the fool will care less about whether or not you know what's really going on. It is very important for you to understand this deception so that you can avoid drama and heartache.

Now let me show you how a fool implements this deception. Let's say you are about to leave a coworker's birthday party early, and a foolish person asks you why. **Your response should be this: "I would have stayed longer, but when I found out that drugs were being used at this party, I knew that it was time for me to go, because I don't do drugs."** Or let's say you are on a date, but you decide to cut the date short, and your date asks why. **Your response should be: "When you said that you are married, I knew that it was time for me to go, because I don't date married people."**

Recognizing the bad signs or red flags can be used like an alarm clock to wake you up and let you know that it is now time for you to leave or stay.

Proverbs 19:13 A foolish son is the calamity of his father: and contentions of a wife are a continual dropping.

Chapter Forty-Three

When a Fool Pretends You Care More about Hurting Them Than Hurting Yourself

You can count on a fool always to seek for an opportunity to make someone's life miserable. That's why Jesus told us to be wise as a serpent and harmless as a dove—so that we will not be deceived by the ploys of a fool. In his time on earth, Jesus encountered foolish people who tried to discredit him by asking foolish questions and making foolish statements, but every time Jesus disarmed the foolish people with wisdom. In this chapter you will see how a fool will pretend that you are so caught up in trying to hurt them that you are willing even to hurt yourself. Now, as Christians, our goal is not to hurt anyone, but to help, and to love everyone with the love of Jesus. The goal of the foolish with this ploy is to harass and annoy you with false accusations that you are trying to hurt them in some way. If they can cause you to act out of character by fearfully trying to convince them that you are not trying to hurt them, then the foolish are very pleased with themselves. The foolish know that your actions were not designed to hurt them, but they don't care; they only care about harassing you.

Now let's see how a fool implements this lie. Here is an example. If your foolish boss accuses you of tearing up the work truck, **this should be your response: "Now why would I tear up the truck and make my job harder, and put my job in jeopardy?"** Here is another example. Let's say your business partner makes a foolish statement, accusing you of not caring about the success of the company. **Your response should be: "Now why would I not care about the success of the company when I have just as much to lose as you do?"**

Knowing how to answer foolish people wisely will always deliver you out of their manipulation and ploys.

Proverbs 21:20 There is treasure to be desired and oil in the dwelling of the wise; but a foolish man spendeth it up.

Chapter Forty-Four

When the Foolish Pretend They Can Solve Their Problems through Their Emotions

This principle is simple but very good in helping people to control their emotion. It will also help you not to be fooled when the foolish pretend they can solve their problems through out-of-control emotion. Granted, we all get emotional about some things, and rightfully so, but foolish people will abuse this fact in order to manipulate or intimidate you into doing what they want you to do. Just like a baby, a fool will try to use emotions to get attention, but for the wrong reason. A fool will use excesses of crying, laughter, sorrow, and anger to further their foolish agenda. That's why it's important to be aware of this form of manipulation, because if you are not, you will fall for the ploy, and—God forbid—possibly be foolish enough to use this ploy on someone else.

So now let's see how this deception is played out. For example, when a foolish person displays extreme anger in regard to a problem that they have, **your response should be, "I understand the problem that you have, but what I don't understand is how you think that losing your temper will somehow fix everything."**

Here is another example. You notice a foolish person displaying signs of depression in regard to a problem that he or she is dealing with. **Your response should be: "I know you have a problem that you are trying to solve, but keep in mind that your problem cannot be fixed by worrying, excessive crying, and sleeping all day; none of those things will help."**

So, as you can see, the goal of the foolish is to deceive you into supporting their foolish agenda by abusing their own emotions, so don't let yourself be fooled. Understand that the fool is just trying intimidate or manipulate you, so be wise.

Proverbs 29:9 If a wise man contendeth with a foolish man, whether he rage or laugh, there is no rest.

Chapter Forty-Five

When the Foolish Act Like They Can Discourage You by Strongly Expressing Their Dislikes

This principle will help you not to be fazed when a foolish person intentionally expresses his or her dislike about you or what you have, because the fool's goal with this ploy is to rob you of your joy and replace it with misery. If you don't understand what's going on, it will be hard for you to stay happy about the things you like, because you will care too much about what people think, and that's exactly what they want you to do—to be overly concerned about what they think. Why should you have to conceal your joy about things that you like, and give people so much power over you? As the Bible says in Proverbs 29:25 the fear of man will prove to be a snare unto you, but thank God it doesn't have to be that way, because Jesus came to set us free. I thank God for the wisdom to know how to respond to this deception, so that a fool will be convinced that it is a waste of time to come at you with this kind of foolishness. Only when you learn how not to answer a fool according to his folly will you be able to maintain your joy concerning the things that appeal to you, as long as they don't offend God.

So now let's see how the foolish implement this ploy. You have just purchased a new car, for example, but your foolish cousin, who is jealous, tells you that he doesn't like it. **Your response should be, "What do you not like about it?"** Asking this question will unexpectedly put pressure on the foolish and convey to them that you are not disturbed by their jealousy. Nine out of ten times, the foolish cousin will not have an answer. Why? Because he really doesn't have an answer; he is just jealous. Here is another example. Let's say you get a promotion on the job, and, out of envy and jealousy, a foolish coworker says to you, "That's not a good position." Here is your response: **"What's not good about the position?"** Again, because the foolish coworker is simply jealous, he will not be able to give you a good reason for his comment. This is a powerful way to respond to statements from foolish people that are based on jealousy.

Proverbs 22:15 Foolishness is bound in the heart of a child; but the rod of correction shall drive it far from him.

Chapter Forty-Six

When a Fool Pretends You Must Be Controlled by a Good or Bad Situation

Foolishness comes in so many different forms that we must not be just one step ahead, but as many steps ahead as possible, because a fool will not stop and wait for you to learn all the different ploys that he or she will use against you. With this ploy the goal is to fool you into thinking that your good or bad situation is so overwhelming that you can't move pass it, when in reality you can and you must move on. That's why it's important to be enlightened about this deception, so that you can avoid being a person who has a hard time letting go of the past, be it good or bad. Granted we all have had some good situations in our lives that we thank God for, and it will do us some good to remember them. Concerning the bad situations, if we do happen to look back, it should only be to remember the lessons that we have learned from them. But a fool will be very happy if he can cause you to stay so wrapped up in your past that you will be too distracted to deal with your present situation, and that's why the scripture says in Philippians 3:13 that we are to forget those things that are behind and reach forward unto those things that are before us. If we don't learn to move on from those good or bad moments in our lives, we will not have the energy to deal with all the new moments that we encounter, so we must be wise and not allow a foolish person to trip us up with this ploy.

Now let's look at how this ploy is used against us. If, for example, a foolish person keeps reminding you of a embarrassing moment you had, your response should be: **"Well, as embarrassing as it was, I thank God because now that it's over, I am a lot wiser and stronger."** Or, for example, if a foolish person keeps talking about how bad your golf game is, this is your response:
"Well, as bad as my golf game is right now, I will be great."
Or let's say a friend becomes foolish and asks you to go bowling during the time that you normally attend church, tempting you with something that you really like to do. Here is your response: **"As much as I like bowling, I like church more."**

Remember that, no matter how good or bad the situation is, you can move on.

190

Conclusion

The greatest level of a fool is a person who doesn't believe in God.

The fool hath said in his heart, there is no God.
—Psalm 14:1

It is our desire that everyone come to know Jesus as their Lord and Savior. And this can be done simply by accepting Jesus into your heart.

Romans 10:9 gives us the instruction that "if thou shalt confess with thy mouth the Lord Jesus, and shalt believe in thine heart that God hath raised him from the dead, thou shalt be saved."

Marlon and Marquinn Carson are identical twin brothers who both serve as ministers in their local church. They both have wonderful wives and kids. In the past fifteen years, under the direction of the Holy Spirit, they have learned forty-six different ways to answer foolish people wisely. These responses have changed them from being quiet and shy and afraid to be themselves and to speak their minds around foolish people, into being wise, bold, and very outspoken. Never again will they fear foolish judgments from foolish people.

www.howtoanswerafool.com
E-mail howtoanswerafool@gmail.com

Made in the USA
Lexington, KY
16 April 2013